"YOU CANNOT TRAVEL ON THE PATH
BEFORE YOU HAVE BECOME THE PATH ITSELF"
GAUTAMA BUDDHA

LENA HERZOG
PILGRIMS
BECOMING THE PATH ITSELF
TEXT BY WERNER HERZOG

FIRST PUBLISHED IN OCTOBER 2002 BY ARCPERIPLUS PUBLISHING LTD,
98 CHURCH ROAD,
LONDON SW13 0DQ,
UNITED KINGDOM

PUBLISHER: DANIÈLE JUNCQUA NAVEAU
DESIGN: KARL HEISELMAN
MANAGING EDITOR: NICHOLAS EASTERBROOK
PRODUCTION MANAGER: SOPHIE CHÉRY
REVISION: HERB GOLDER, NICHOLAS EASTERBROOK

ISBN 1-902699-43-2

SCANNING AND REPROGRAPHICS, PERIPLUS PUBLISHING LONDON LTD
FILM PROCESSING, FLESHTONE COLOR LAB
PRINTED IN ITALY BY GRAPHICOM, VICENZA

LENA HERZOG
PILGRIMS

BECOMING THE PATH ITSELF

TEXT BY WERNER HERZOG

The pictures in this book were taken in Bodhgaya in the State of Bihar/India and around Mount Kailash in Western Tibet, arguably the two most holy sites in the Buddhist world.

In January 2002, Bodhgaya was chosen by His Holiness, the Dalai Lama, for the performance of the highly important Kalachakra Initiation ceremonies, which are held at irregular intervals every few years at an assigned site. Bodhgaya is a village with a few thousand inhabitants which hosted an estimated half million pilgrims for the planned Kalachakra Initiation. Only recently has the Kalachakra Initiation taken place outside areas with a deeply rooted Buddhist culture. It has been held at Madison/Wisconsin, Zurich, Los Angeles, New York, Barcelona, Sydney and Bloomington/Indiana. Graz/Austria will be only the eighth city in the western world to witness the Kalachakra ritual.

Mount Kailash is considered the spiritual and physical centre of the universe, a mountain of the highest significance not only for Buddhists, but also for Hindus, Jain, and the shamanistic Tibetan Bon-Po religion, which dates back to pre-Buddhist times. Since 2002 happens to be a year of the horse, occurring every twelve years, the pilgrimage around Kailash, the Kora, rewards the faithful with twelve times the deliverance of sins. Because of this auspicious date, tens of thousands of pilgrims will make the journey. During other months or years there would only be an irregular trickle of the faithful.

Both these places and events are only seemingly unrelated. Yet the focal point of the Kalachakra Initiation is a highly symbolic and complicated sand mandala which is laid out around the symbol of Mount Kailash, the centre of the world. The mountain itself is not only a very impressive pyramid of black rock with a cap of ice and snow on its top, it immediately strikes the voyager as something much deeper – an inner landscape, an apparition of something existing only in the soul of man. Pilgrims, whether you meet them en route to Santiago de Compostela, to the shrine of the Virgin de Guadalupe in Tepeyac, Mexico, or anywhere else, seem to be a metaphor for human life. Their devotion, their fervour, their suffering, their prayers are written on their faces, whether they be Catholics, Hindus or Buddhists. Their sojourn in the flesh, seeking a spiritual goal, has the quality of something universal, purely metaphorical: our course of mortal life figured as a journey.

But, walking with them, climbing a 19 000-foot high pass in a hailstorm, left alone with one's breath, aching chest and laden shoulders among all the others equally reduced to breathing and praying, makes one thing beyond the metaphor clear: this is life, life in its quintessential form – *pura vida*. Follow a woman who has walked a couple of thousand miles all the way from Tibet to Bodhgaya with her infant on her back, moving among the crowd at the village market. Bare feet, dirt beyond description, garbage, pushing, shoving, noise from rickshaws and loudspeakers. The woman bends over, vomits, and walks on praying. A big, fat, greasy rat right next to her does the same – bends over, vomits – but then it rolls over on its side and dies.

10 And then there is a tall, ascetic monk from the province of Amdo, beyond the Tibetan Autonomous Region, who has arrived after a journey of over three thousand kilometres lasting more than three years, prostrating himself all the way to Bodhgaya. His wrists have grown nodes, and there is a spot in the middle of his forehead, a crusted wound which does not heal. He has touched the ground with his forehead millions of times, each time advancing no more than the length of his body. Standing, he radiates the placidity of a statue. Dignity hovers around him like an aura. Faith? Prayers? He does not want to speak about it. Heat? Yes, heat. Thirst? Great thirst. But sometimes, as word spread of his coming, nomads approached and gave him water and something to eat. And the distance? Yes, he knows how big the earth is. How big? He has measured it with his body, he knows. The mountains are high and the desert is vast. He moved on and he has arrived.

The average mortal arrives by train, in the depths of night on a hopelessly overcrowded train from Delhi after twenty hours along the vast Ganges valley. The train stops in the middle of fields, at towns where more people and hungry children crowd and scramble into the wagons, followed by hordes of monkeys who steal sun-glasses and a pack of unfiltered cigarettes before fleeing. The city of Gaya's station lurks in the dark. Shouting, more scrambling and the train spews pilgrims out into the night. Stepping over bundles and sleeping travellers on the platform you reach the arrival hall, which is filled from corner to corner with hundreds upon hundreds of huddled people.

They sleep on the ground, body next to body, wrapped in rugs and thin blankets. Others are sitting sleeplessly. You step through waves of humanity followed by a silent ocean of eyes.

The town of Bodhgaya is now some twelve miles away. Wandering for years as an itinerant ascetic, Buddha finally rested here under a tree and meditated, finding enlightenment. After 2 500 years, the tree is still there, indifferent as all nature toward the travails of men. It is sprouting in its fourth or fifth generation; its vast old branches supported by poles. Under its shadow thousands of monks pray in endless litanies, sitting disciplined in lotus position. All of a sudden, wild movement tosses some rows into disarray: a leaf has fallen from the tree and amidst the sudden scramble a blissful young monk has caught it. Till the end of his life – this life, as he points out – the leaf is the greatest gift he will ever receive. He feels blessed. A Great Treasure has come upon him.

The village of Bodhgaya can be made out from miles away as half a million pilgrims swirl dust into the air. Bodhgaya itself has vanished under a grey, cloud-like torpor, and from the distance a great veil hovers in the air, motionless, suffocating. Eyes turn red, and throats become sore. Entering one of the vast makeshift tent-cities around Bodhgaya there is hoarse coughing everywhere. Thousands wear face-masks and after a few days it is hundreds of thousands. Many weep, their eyes infected. On the first day of the Kalachakra ceremonies, hundreds can be seen lining up outside the tents which tend to the sick. There are makeshift hospitals and pharmacies, most of them treating patients according to Tibetan traditional medicine, and a few days later the end of the queues loses itself somewhere in the shoving crowds in the distance. And yet there is an air of joy and elation among the sick.

An amusement park has sprung up with a few, sad, hand-driven carousels, as well as a lottery, a half-lame rollercoaster limping empty in its rusty tracks, balloons, and a balding monkey, itching from scabies, who does The Somersault (backwards). In a separate tent there are Siamese twins, who attract quite a few of the curious. Two young men in their twenties, joined inseparably at the hips, look silently back at the onlookers and seem to start at the attempt by a Thai monk in saffron to talk to them. Blaring loudspeakers everywhere, honking cars and rickshaws ringing their bells. Almost every stand which has sprung up along the roads has its own blaring music, more noisy and further from high fidelity than anything you have ever heard. But India has no concept of noise. It is the destined confession of life.

And then there are oases of silence. Around the stupa, a tall shrine next to the Tree of Enlightenment, the prayers are silent or merely murmured, and only a few falcons, denizens of the crags in the stone adornments, screech in flight. Prayer flags flutter in the wind. In a corner next to them burn thousands of butter lamps, which all sizzle softly when a draught of air worries the flames. Outside, merchants sell small birds who are so densely crammed into their cages that

they have fallen silent, and only when a hand stirs them to get one out, do they twitter in their little anxiety and then fall silent again. A Mongolian monk has bought two tiny birds and releases them. They whirr from his hands before they are half open. Each being should have the chance to be reborn into a higher existence, he says, but you can achieve this only when you are free. He stands for a long time and smiles, and does not see that the birds are recaught by barefoot boys to be sold again.

Bodhgaya has also attracted a crowd of beggars, Untouchables. They line every sidewalk, crouching on the ground, pleading for alms. Stumps of arms and festering hands without fingers, all claimed by leprosy, are stretched towards the pilgrims and they, the beggars, seem to be some other manifestation, a spectral apparition of the pilgrims themselves. Pilgrims from another life, from another world, where street urchins crawl on the ground and children mutilated by their parents are sent out begging. Half pilgrim, half crab, they move amongst the feet of the crowds. Their hopelessness makes you shudder and you wish this were only an ostentation from some science fiction, not of the future, but of a distant past.

From the first day on, after solemn ceremonies and a dance performed by masked dancers, a team of Tibetan monks works on the Kalachakra sand mandala, the focal point of the Kalachakra ceremonies. It is a highly complicated symbolic representation of the wheel of time, so complex that there are five volumes of scriptures of instructions, and two hundred and four volumes of commentary and exegesis. Making it even more labyrinthine, these are disputed among the main lineages of Buddhist faith. In principle it is the dwelling of a Buddha, the representation of a three-dimensional palace on the summit of Mount Kailash. It should be visualised as a pyramid with its tip resting on the summit of the mountain. The artists come from the monastery of the Dalai Lama in Dharamsala, and these monks work in shifts around the clock with only four hours of rest during the wee hours of the night. The blueprint is delineated on a platform, and four monks lay out the image with very fine sand of different colours. They squat on the four sides of the platform working with the utmost concentration. The sand is laid out through needle-fine funnels, soft knocks to the sides of which cause the sand to trickle with pinpoint precision. The monks wear face-masks. To breathe on the mandala, to sneeze or cough would spell disaster.

The Dalai Lama is supposed to ceremoniously lay the first line of the mandala, but he has fallen ill and cannot appear. In an instant, Bodhgaya is filled with whispers, prayers and rumours. How ill is His Holiness? How ill is he really, the day's medical bulletin notwithstanding? Will he be able to perform the ceremonies? And there is a suppressed question on everyone's mind: what will happen if he dies? The unthinkable has sunk into everyone's heart. Tens of thousands hold a prayer vigil throughout the night. Tired and hollow-eyed monks fall asleep during the endless hours of teaching and instruction during the day. The noise of Bodhgaya has scaled

down. A blanket of dull, resigned stupor covers the stumbling crowds. Large throngs of silent pilgrims wait at the gate of the monastery where the Dalai Lama resides. They cannot be persuaded to leave.

Around the stupa at the Bodhi tree the congregations of monks continue their litanies. The circumambulation of the sacred place on three levels proceeds. A never-ending stream of thousands and thousands pushes on. Everyone leaves shoes and sandals behind at the bottom. Many circle the inner sanctum measuring their length in prostrations. Huge glowing piles of incense fumigate the faithful. Hundreds of beggars' hands stretch through the fence toward the pilgrims and on the day of alms the beggars fall into a frenzy. Young monks have laid out wooden planks in two corners of the inner area and prostrate themselves one hundred thousand times. Over a four-week period, the wood on the floor becomes shiny and polished from the sliding of bodies and hands. Faith is beyond dissuasion, belief does not stagger.

The vast area for the monks' instruction fills up every morning and afternoon. The highest lamas of the four main lineages of Tibetan Buddhism perform the teachings. But the throne of the Dalai Lama remains unoccupied. During short breaks, young novices sprint outside to the immense cauldrons where butter tea has been prepared, fill their teapots and scramble for the honour of serving their group of monks first. They run back again and again, robes fluttering, bumping into each other. So wild is the rush on the steaming cauldrons that stout monks with no-nonsense faces keep the pushing and shoving under control, using their bamboo sticks to beat back the most tumultuous. Tea spills on to the ground. Laughter, joyful scolding. Flat, round bread is distributed in baskets. The bread is still warm from the ovens and while the monks eat, dozens of monk-bakers knead the dough for a hundred thousand more loaves.

On the fifth day there is an announcement that His Holiness, the Dalai Lama, will appear in public. The onrush of crowds is so enormous that workers have to take down part of the outer fences. The Dalai Lama is greeted with boundless fervour, with vehement devotion. His voice is warm as he speaks in Tibetan. He will not be able to perform the endless hours of ceremonies, he is too frail, he is deeply sorry that he has to cancel the Kalachakra Initiation. Yet the teachings will continue, the sand mandala will be made accessible for the pilgrims and the Long Life Ceremony will be held.

During this ceremony a sort of small dumpling made of barley is handed out, and it is considered particularly auspicious to receive one of these at the occasion of the Kalachakra ceremonies. Wherever young monks appear with their basket, instant tumult breaks out. Finding yourself in the middle of this bedlam is a dangerous experience, as a maelstrom of bodies sucks you into a vortex around the basket, and many who get trampled underfoot in the raging tempest of bodies suffer serious injury.

After this the atmosphere seems to deflate. Pilgrims from Thailand, Burma, Bhutan and Japan are the first to make travel arrangements. Tibetan monks crowd the tiny internet cafes to send e-mails. Only for the yak nomads from inner Tibet does the message sink in more slowly. For them, time the devourer of things sets down its noiseless foot with greater wariness. Next day, all of the pilgrims queue up for the mandala. At five in the morning, the queue is already a mile long, body to body. Silence. No pushing, no shoving, nobody speaks. When an old Tibetan yak-herder carrying his mother on his back lines up, he is quietly motioned forward with his burden. The old woman creases her parchment face into even more wrinkles and smiles.

The same archetypal image on the way to Mount Kailash. A battered truck overflowing with pilgrims stops by a creek. Small fires of dried yak-dung glow, their life kindled by simple goatskin bellows. Before the last man, a nomad with his old mother on his back, has climbed down, tea with rancid butter and a few handfuls of barley flour is being prepared in battered teapots. Trucks are heading west for the sacred mountain; fifty, sixty pilgrims are crammed together for their relentless journey through dust, the bitter cold of the mornings, and the scorching heat of the day. All faces are covered with a piece of cloth and sun-glasses which seem to come from a different century. Some pilgrims resemble spectres, having masked their faces with white linen, leaving only two holes for eyes. Bundles, water containers and rolled-up blankets are hung around the trucks and bounce through potholes in the same rhythm as the pilgrims. Flags flutter on poles. The pilgrims sing.

The land is vast and solitary, no trees, no vegetation, and you wonder how roaming herds of yaks, antelope and wild asses can survive. With the snow-covered chain of the Himalayas to the south, the immense spaces of inner Tibet barely ever sink below 15 000 feet. When a nomad walks away, you can still see him at midday, and you still see him by nightfall, and next day with a pair of binoculars you still see him as a dot in the landscape. Eagles soar in the crisp, thin air. A hailstorm approaches from the depths of the landscape, passes you in less than a minute, and moves on into infinity. A grey wolf strolls next to the road, which has fanned out into barely visible tracks. The wolf does not run from those closing in on him, does not accelerate his ambling pace. He looks on with a mixture of suspicion, hunger and contempt. Even at these altitudes you will receive the same contempt from a pair of cranes by a river who refuse to be disturbed by a mortal human. And there are still seagulls at over 17 000 feet.

After days of being tossed around in a four-wheel drive, with dust in your ears, nostrils and throat, having crossed high passes in snow, rivers on ancient ferries, crossed desolate plains and stony deserts, the prayer flags of the first prostration point come into sight. From here, Mount Kailash is visible in the distance for the first time. The mountain is the dwelling of the Buddha Demchog (in Tibetan), or Heruka (in Sanskrit), and his consort. For Hindus it is home to the god Shiva and his consort Parvati. The snow-covered peak glistens in the sunlight. The pyramid of dark rock stands in majestic solitude.

But the really striking thing about the mountain is the entire landscape ensemble: Mount Gurla Mandhata towering over 25 000 feet in the south and the two big lakes in between the glaciers and neighbouring peaks of the Himalayas create a unique landscape drama full of hieroglyphic mystery. The larger Lake Manasarovar is considered particularly sacred and is believed to be the embodiment of the forces of light, whereas Lake Rakas Tal represents the dark forces. All the elements combine in a theatre of solemn ecstasy. And when dark cloud banks enshroud the grand ballroom of the spirits, something almost hysterical is manifest.

A monastery between the two lakes, Chiu Gompa, which faces the southern flank of Mount Kailash, was for many years the home of Padmasambhava (or Guru Rinpoche), the saint who introduced Buddhism from India to Tibet during the eighth century AD. He ended his earthly existence by dissolving into the light of a rainbow.

As one approaches the small town of Darchen at the foot of Mount Kailash, the whole area seems to be covered by snow. At a closer distance it turns out to be an entire city of white tents, interspersed with an occasional nomad tent made from dark yak wool. Pilgrims from all over Tibet are camping here. Women wear distinctive traditional costumes, and some of the dialects are so obscure that Tibetans themselves have a hard time understanding each other. Truckload after truckload of pilgrims arrives, covered with dust, tired, but full of joyful elation. They assemble for the annual Sakya Dawa festival on

Buddha's birthday. A big new pole with prayer flags will be erected, and tens of thousands of pilgrims attend, cheering, throwing handfuls of paper with prayers and good wishes into the gusty wind, and going wild when the new mast sways up. It is considered ill-omened if it leans toward the mountain and even more unpropitious if it leans away from it, but this year, as it is pulled up with heavy ropes, it stands straight, or almost straight. Boundless jubilation, prostrations, an onrush of the faithful who try to rip fragments of bark from the mast until uniformed Chinese policemen move in to protect the stem. It will be a very auspicious year. Some pilgrims toss handfuls of barley flour at each other until they are all covered in white.

Half an hour later the site is almost empty. The pilgrims hasten to start the Kora, the circumambulation of Mount Kailash. During the pilgrimage around Mount Kailash, the faithful of the Bon are easily recognisable; they make the circumambulation counter-clockwise, whereas Buddhists and Hindus take the opposite route. Trekking alongside the Buddhists, whoever comes towards you is therefore Bon or the occasional invalid, helped out along the shortest way. The day of the full moon in May, being the birthday of Buddha and anniversary of his enlightenment, attracts the highest number of pilgrims.

Soon, the crowds stretch out in an endless thread of prayers, and hope, and fervour. Yaks carry loads, dogs follow, small children hasten along. Hindus from the lowlands of the Indian subcontinent sweat and toil along. As physical exercise is not part of their culture, almost all are utterly unprepared for the strenuous exertion at such an altitude. As a matter of fact, two of them will die from altitude sickness and an elderly German tourist in critical condition has to be put into a compression tent. Soon some of the weakest will be heaved on to the backs of small, sturdy horses and taken out. But this constitutes only the tiniest fraction of participants: the Tibetans, accustomed to the altitude, move on vigorously. There are very few monks; almost all the pilgrims are nomadic yak-herders with dark tanned faces and wild unkempt hair who sleep exposed to the night. They huddle together in lumps at the bottom of a ditch in open ground, barely covered by some shaggy sheepskin and their shaggy dogs, who also seek the faint ember of bodily warmth. In the morning they will wake up under a thin layer of freshly fallen snow.

Some of the most fervent pilgrims do the circuit of fifty-two kilometres by prostrating themselves all the way. They cross talus, and snowfields, and gravel, and rock, and creeks filled with ice-cold, torrential water. They wear coarse aprons and protect their hands with pieces of wood. It will take them about three weeks to complete the circuit. The hardest part comes after leaving the north flank of Mount Kailash. The mountain here is even more black and towering and forbidding. It is the embodiment of sheer denial. The path climbs up to the Dolma La pass with an elevation of almost 19 000 feet. Up there, an ocean of prayer flags is tugged and ripped in the storm. The pilgrims rest. From there, the path zig-zags down between large

16 boulders. A barely tamed yak takes the opportunity to swipe its load against a boulder and shed it. It immediately departs at full gallop with some nomads and dogs in pursuit.

There are special stations en route: a rock with Buddha's footprint on it, a column of rock with healing powers, over which pilgrims lean their bodies in prayer. Some of them rub their stomachs against the stone and rest bent over the rock for a long time. A child lama, the reincarnation of a very high lama, hastens by on horseback. He is dressed in silk and elaborate adornments, and kept warm with woollen shawls. A large entourage of retainers follows. Trombones blare, prayer wheels are kept in motion, and a framed photo of the boy is being carried in the vanguard. Toward the end of the trek there is a cave connected with the saint Milarepa, high up on the eastern face of the mountain. About a millennium ago he lived here for many years as an ascetic and is believed to have reached enlightenment in a single lifetime. His cave was too small for a human body and thus the saint lay on his back and, pushing up with his feet, raised the rock above. His footprints are said to be visible on the ceiling. After a dispute with a Bon master, which he won, he reached the summit of Mount Kailash by riding on a ray of the sun.

On returning to the starting point, the tent city at Darchen is almost gone and in the distance huge clouds of dust mark the departing trucks on the vast plain towards Lake Manasarovar. Seagulls sail in the cold wind. They must have flown a long way from the sea to reach such a forbidding elevation. Mount Kailash is a geographical enigma, as within a perimeter of a few miles the four biggest rivers of the Indian subcontinent or their tributaries originate: the Ganges, the Sutlej, the Indus and the Brahmaputra. Follow any of the rivers in any direction and you will reach the Indian Ocean. Many miles away, on the return journey, a sudden snow shower blankets the landscape in white. The car has to stop for repairs. Close at hand, the eyes of a fox who has let himself be snowed in watch you. It does not budge as you approach, and only when you are about to step on it, does the animal decide to stir and, unafraid, get up. It stretches leisurely and then, full of arrogance, moves away. The Tibetan driver takes some time to have tea and to fix a leak in the radiator. Then the engine of the four-wheel drive turns over and the car moves on. Kailash, the mountain of attraction and denial, remains behind in marmoreal repose; pure, imperious and without mercy like all principles of the spirit. It glistens and, full of condescension, dismisses the passage of men and the passage of time.

Werner Herzog, June 2002

20

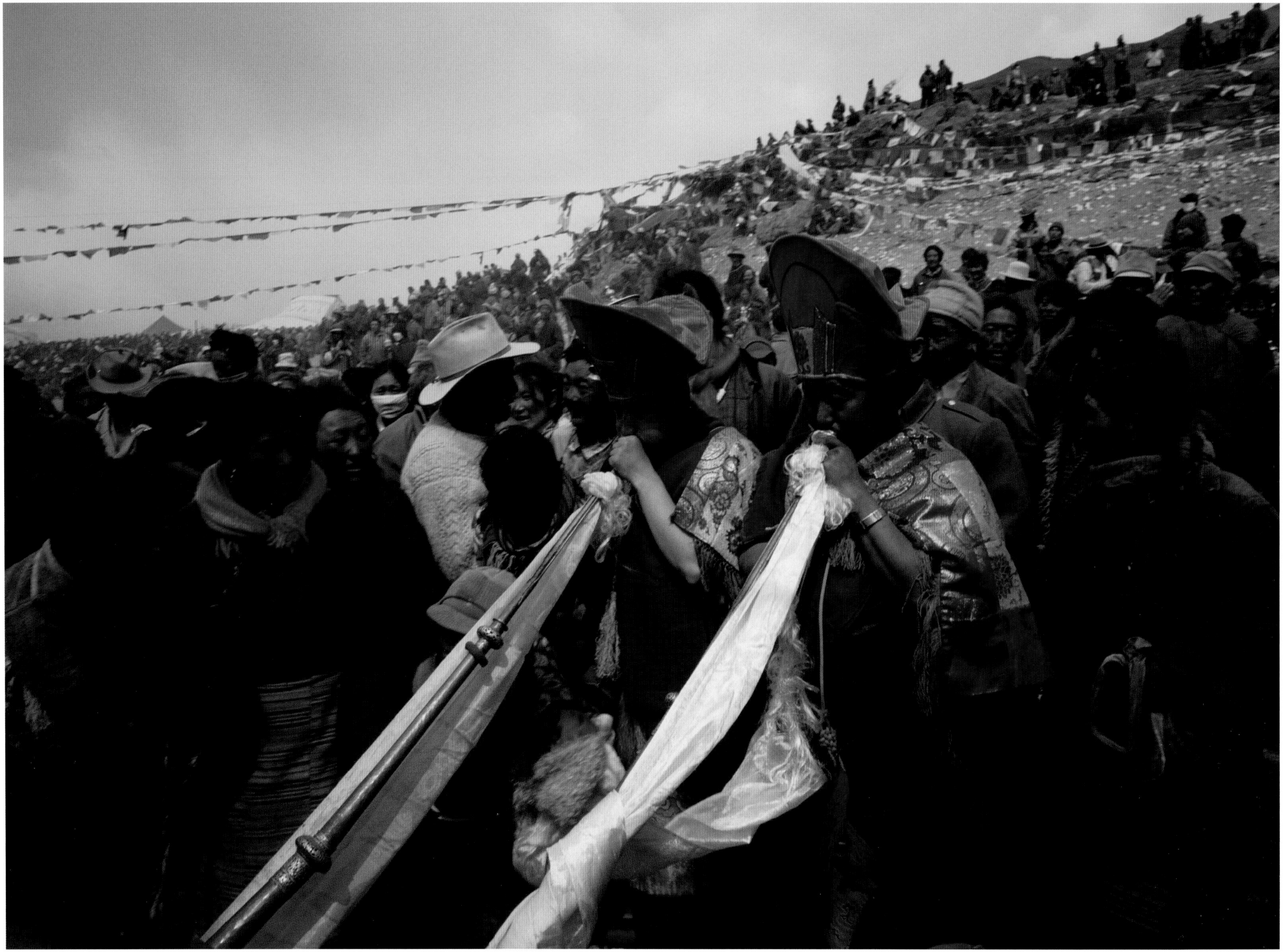

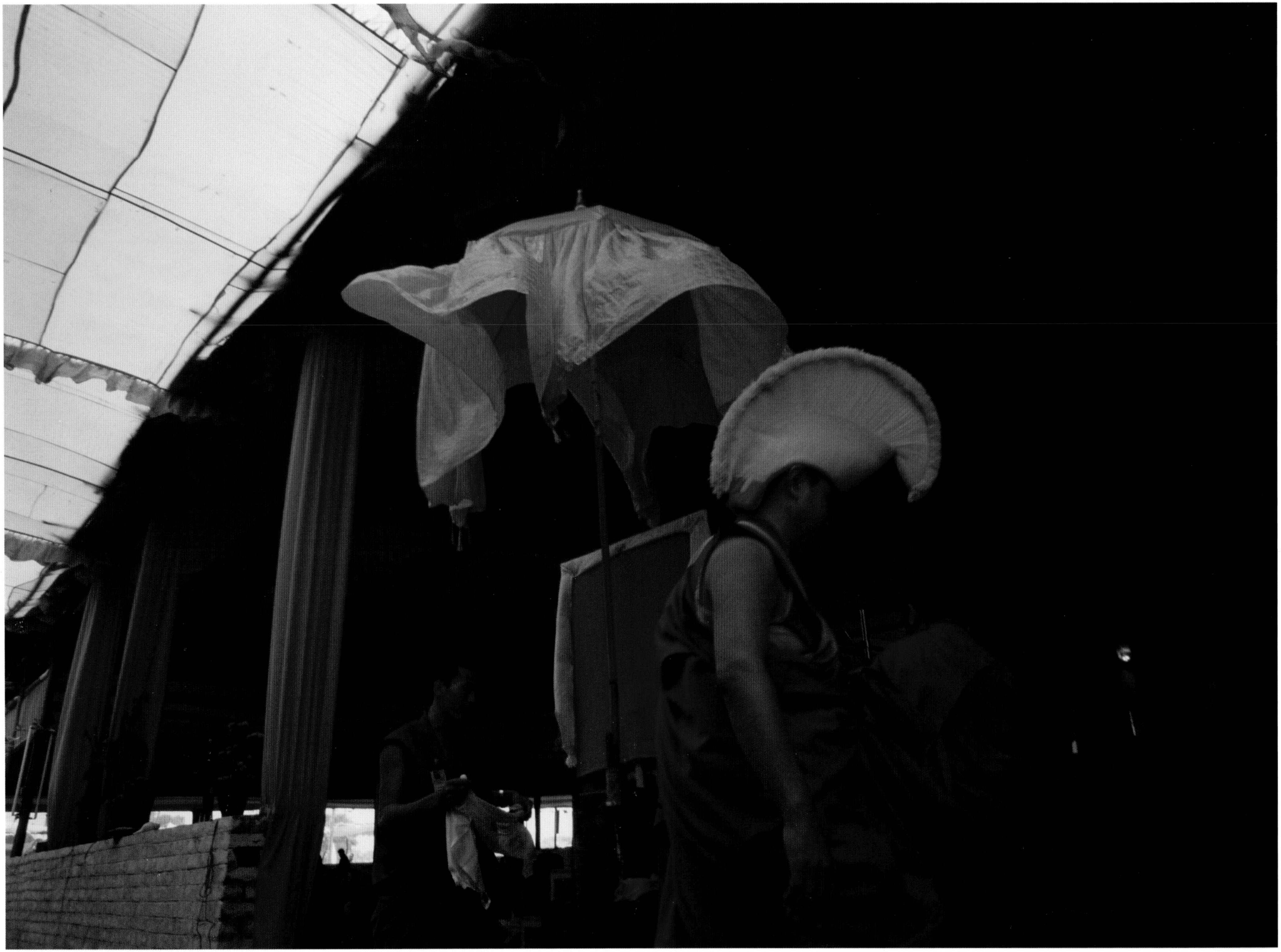

34

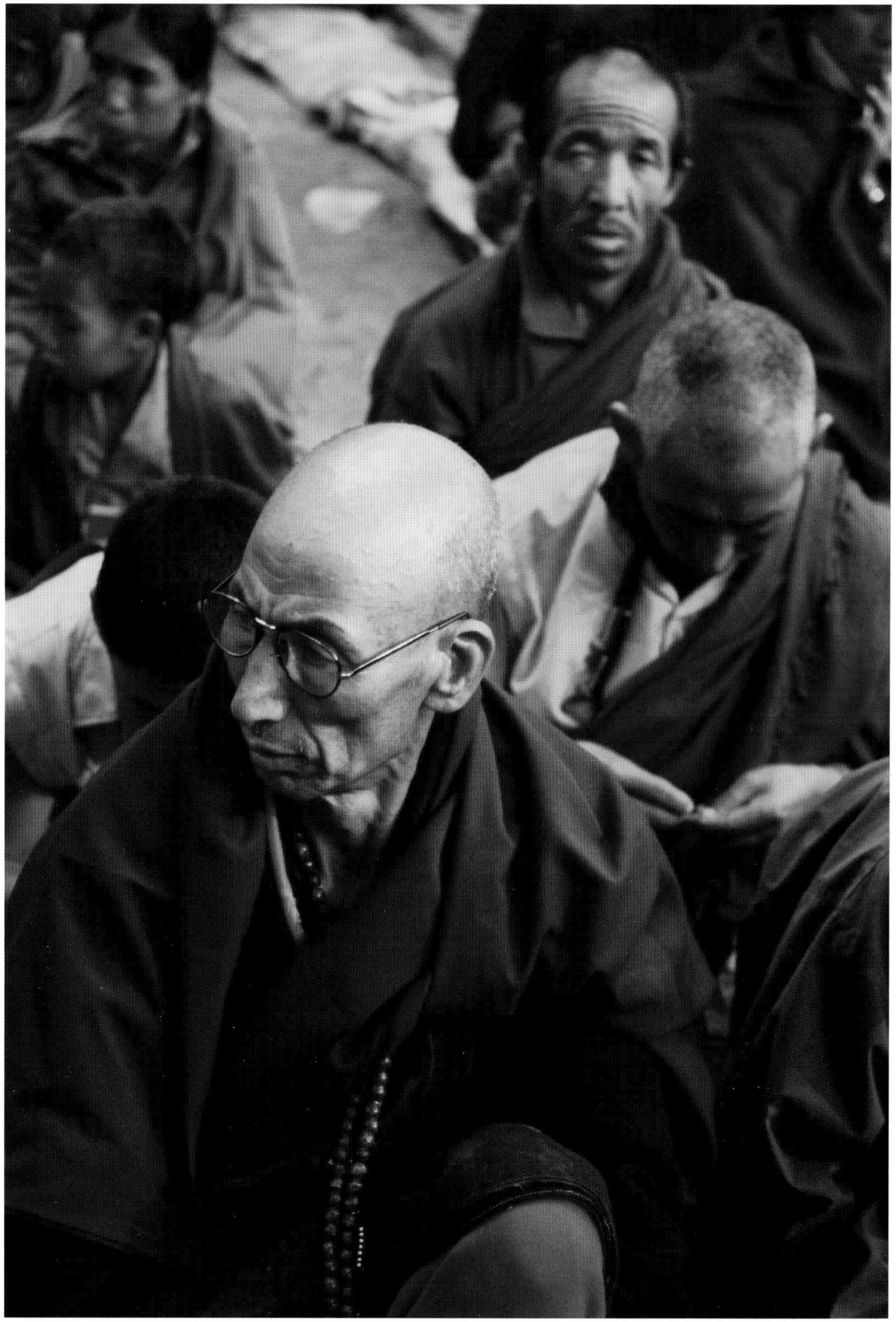

44

48

53

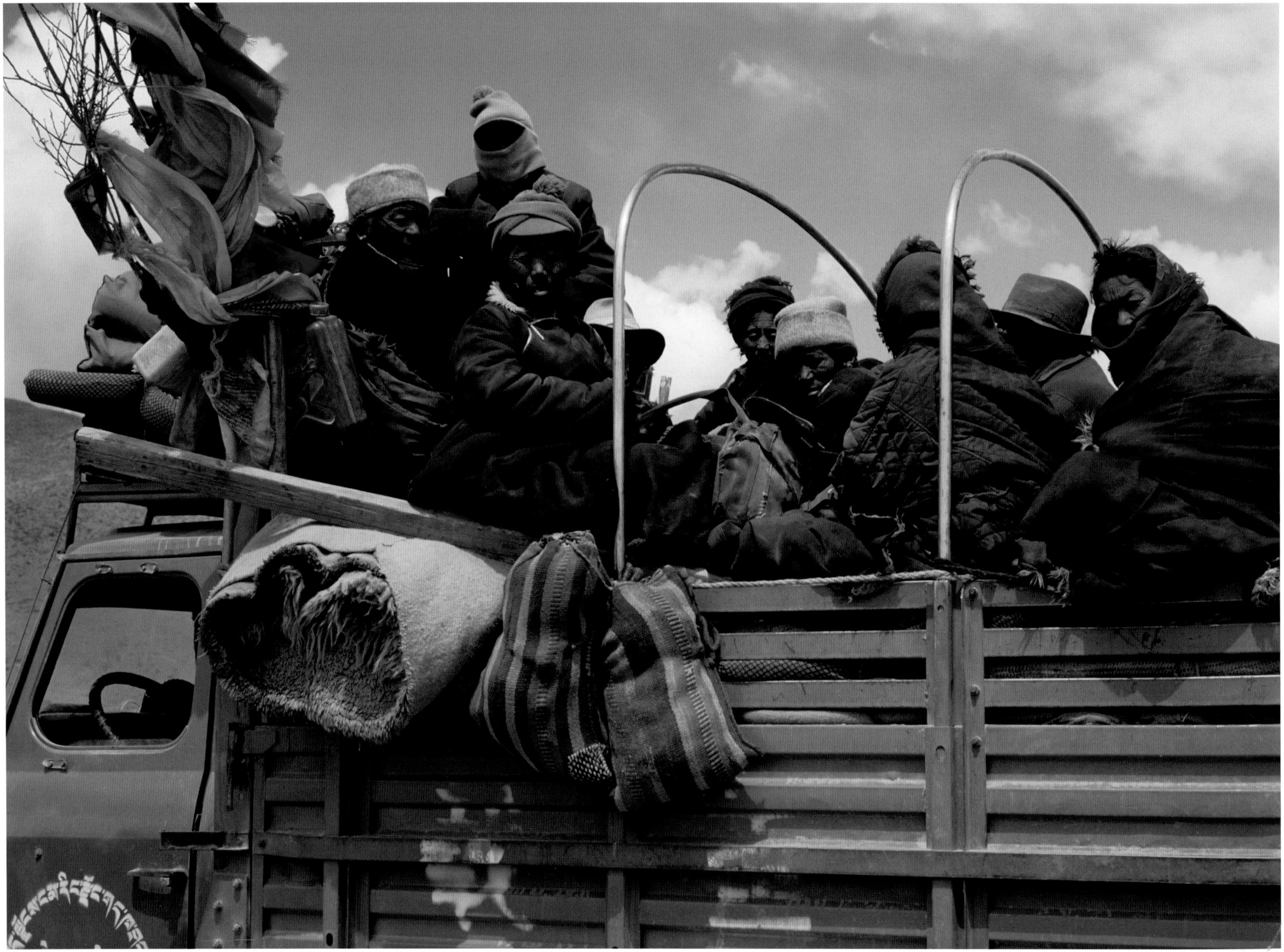

71

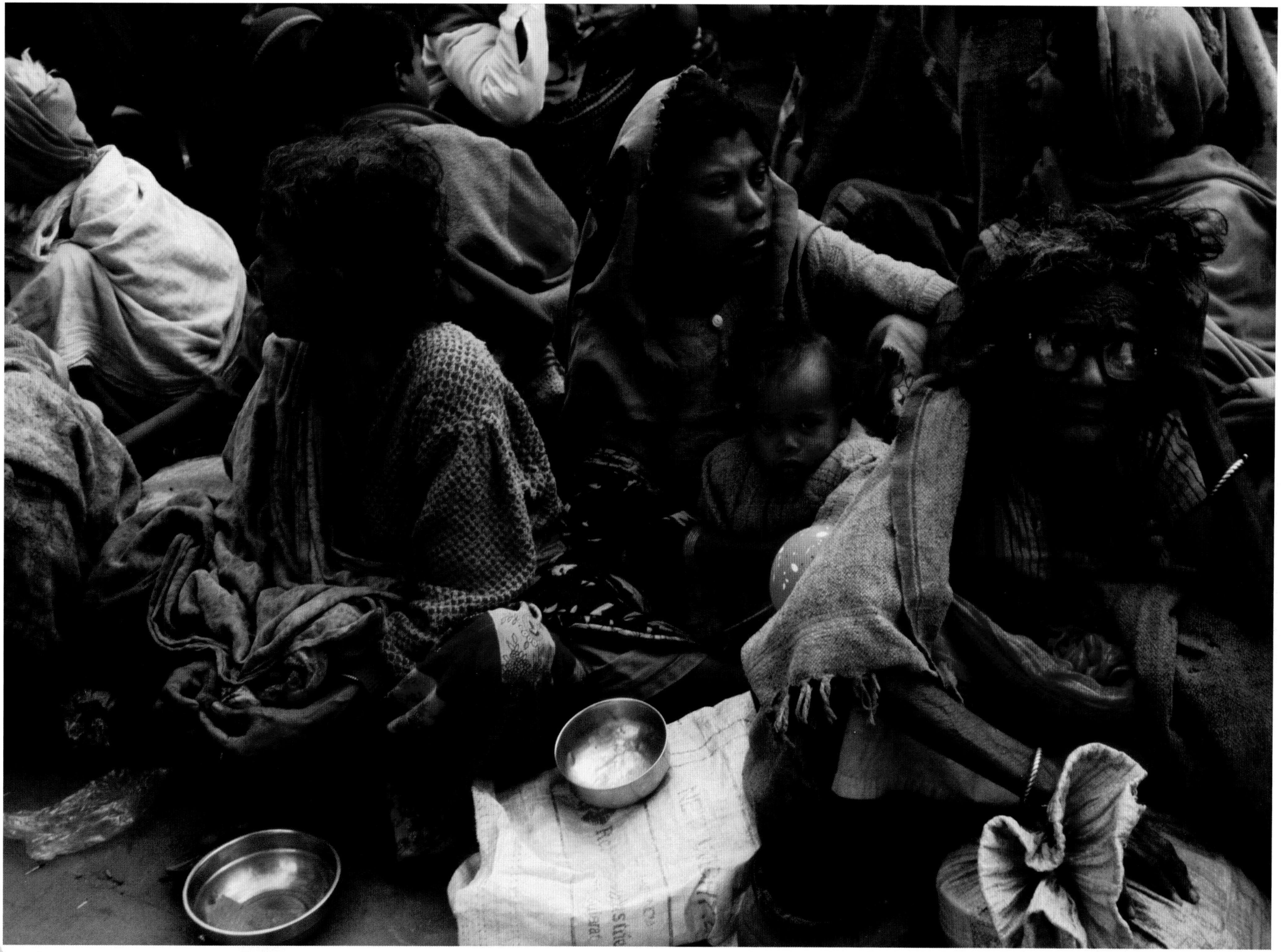

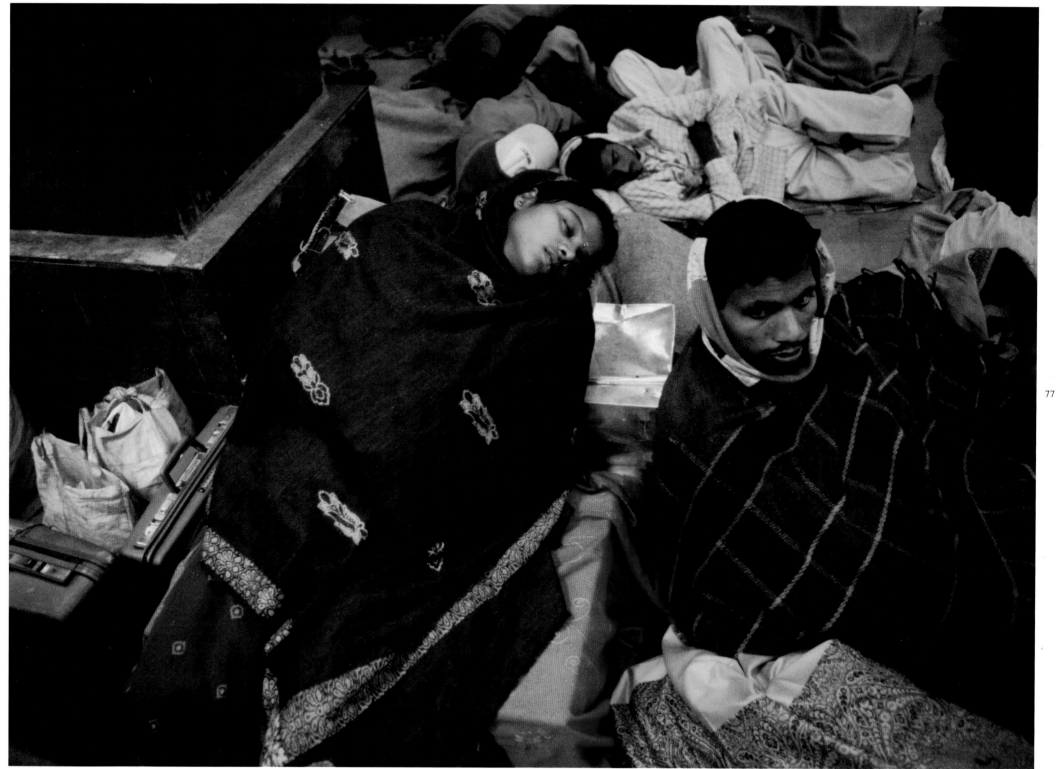

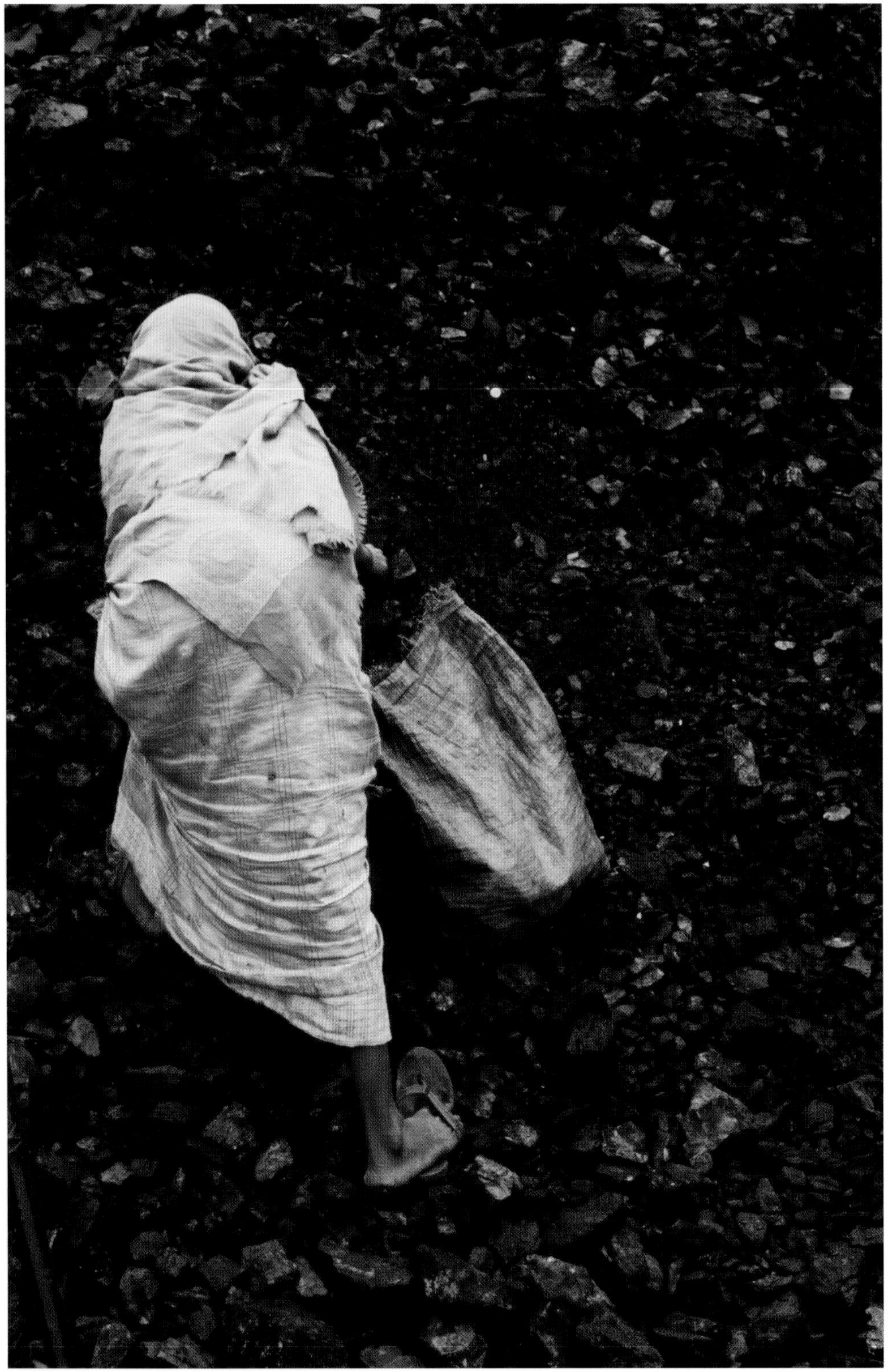

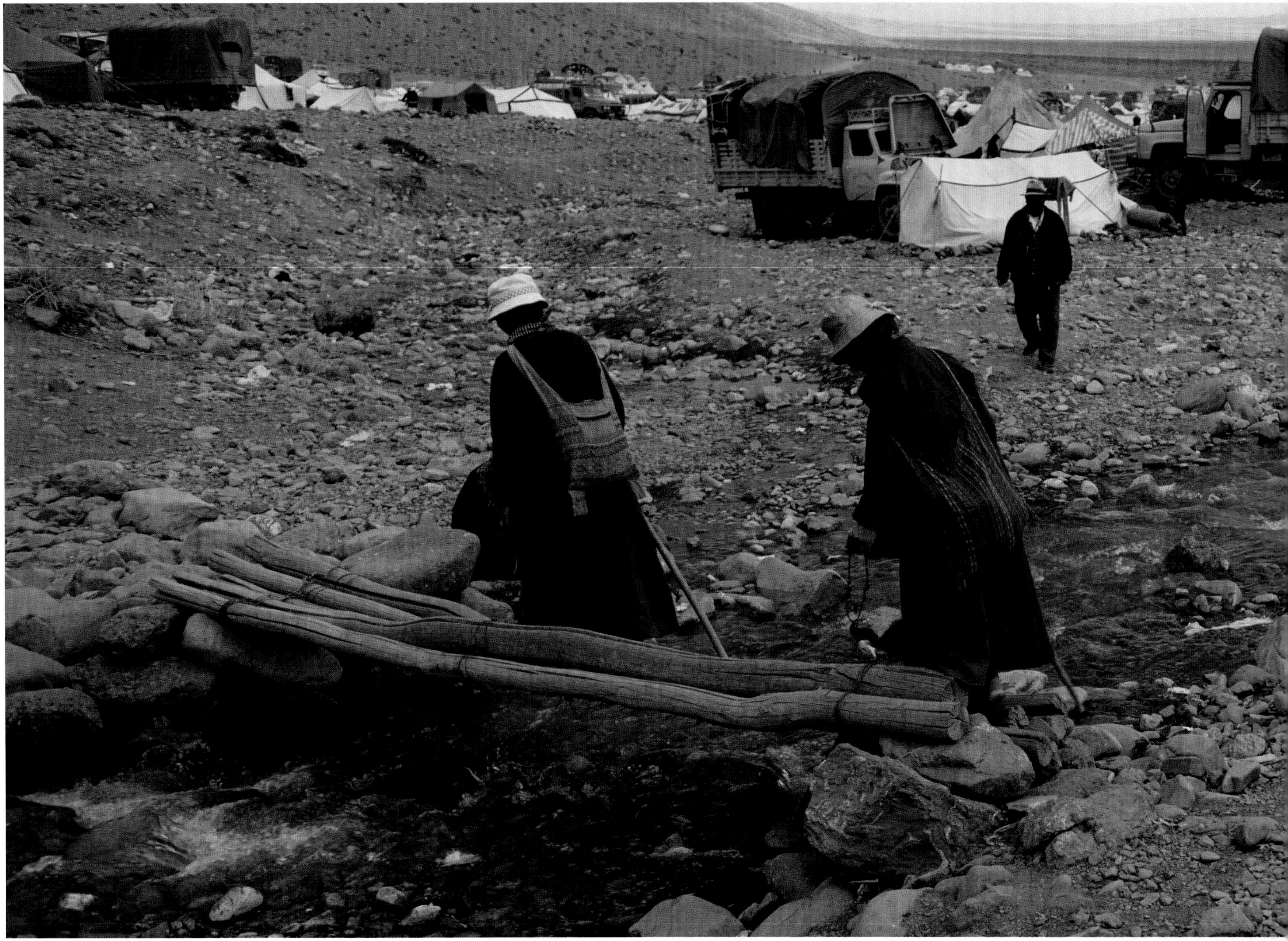

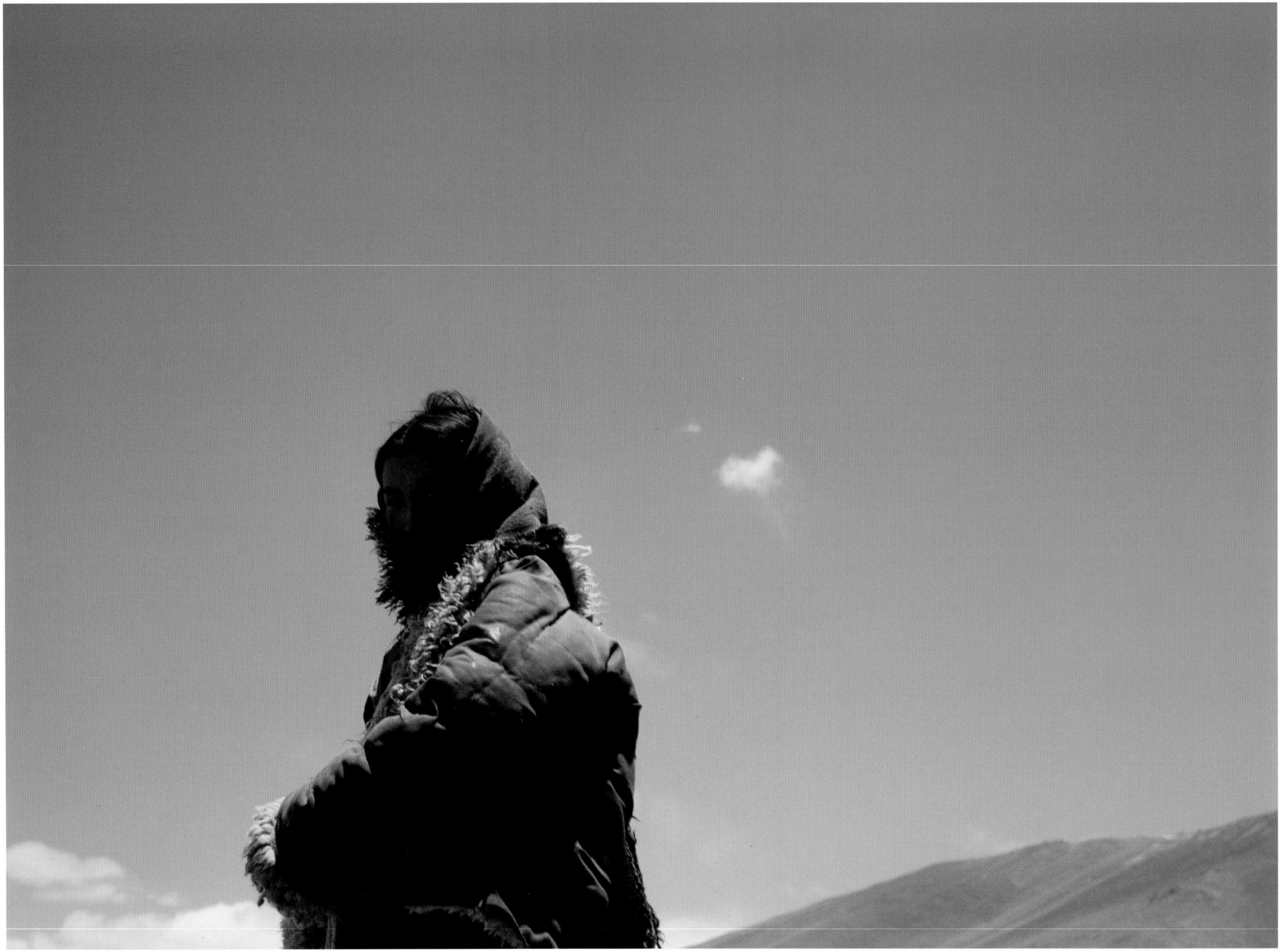

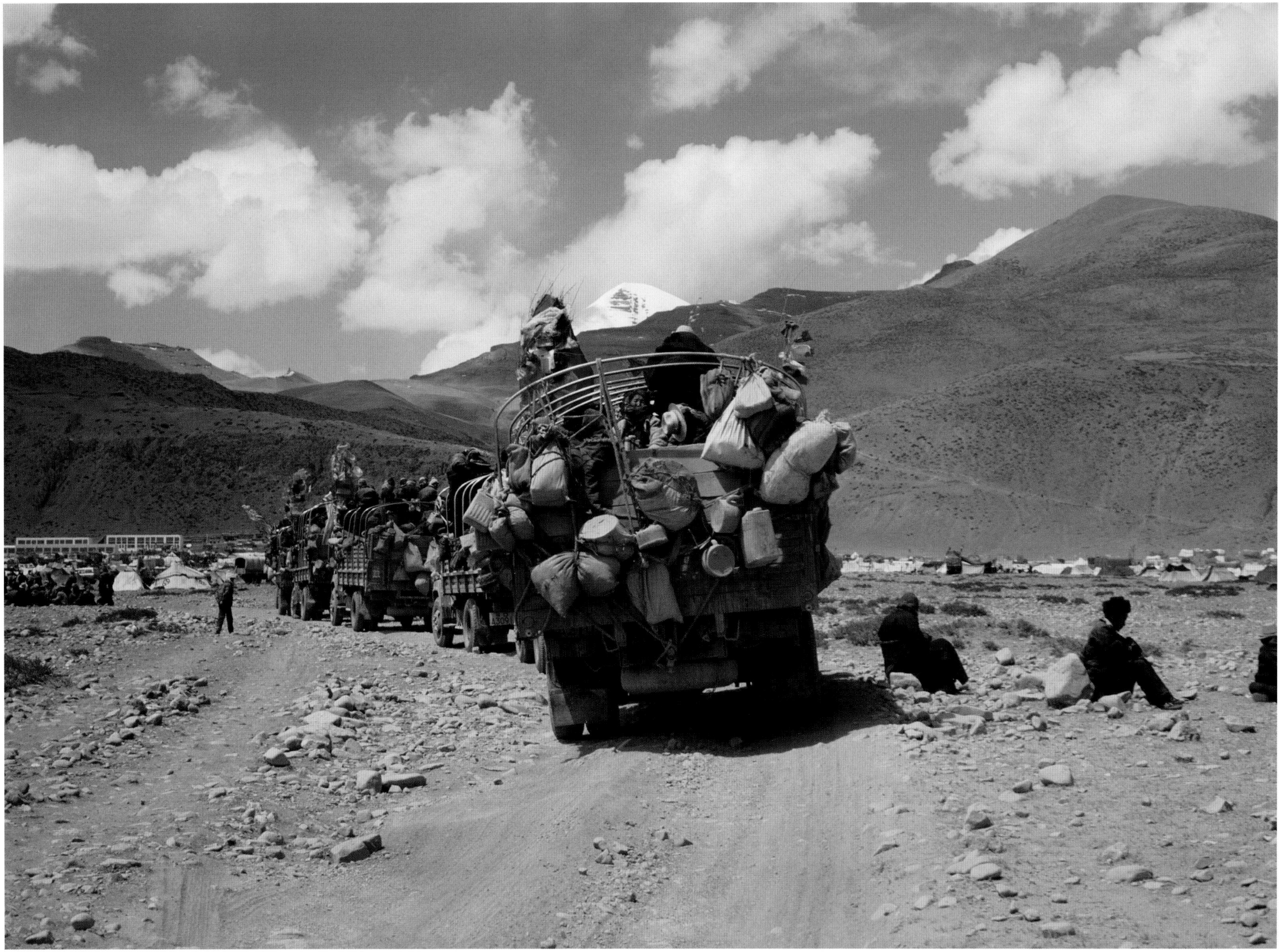

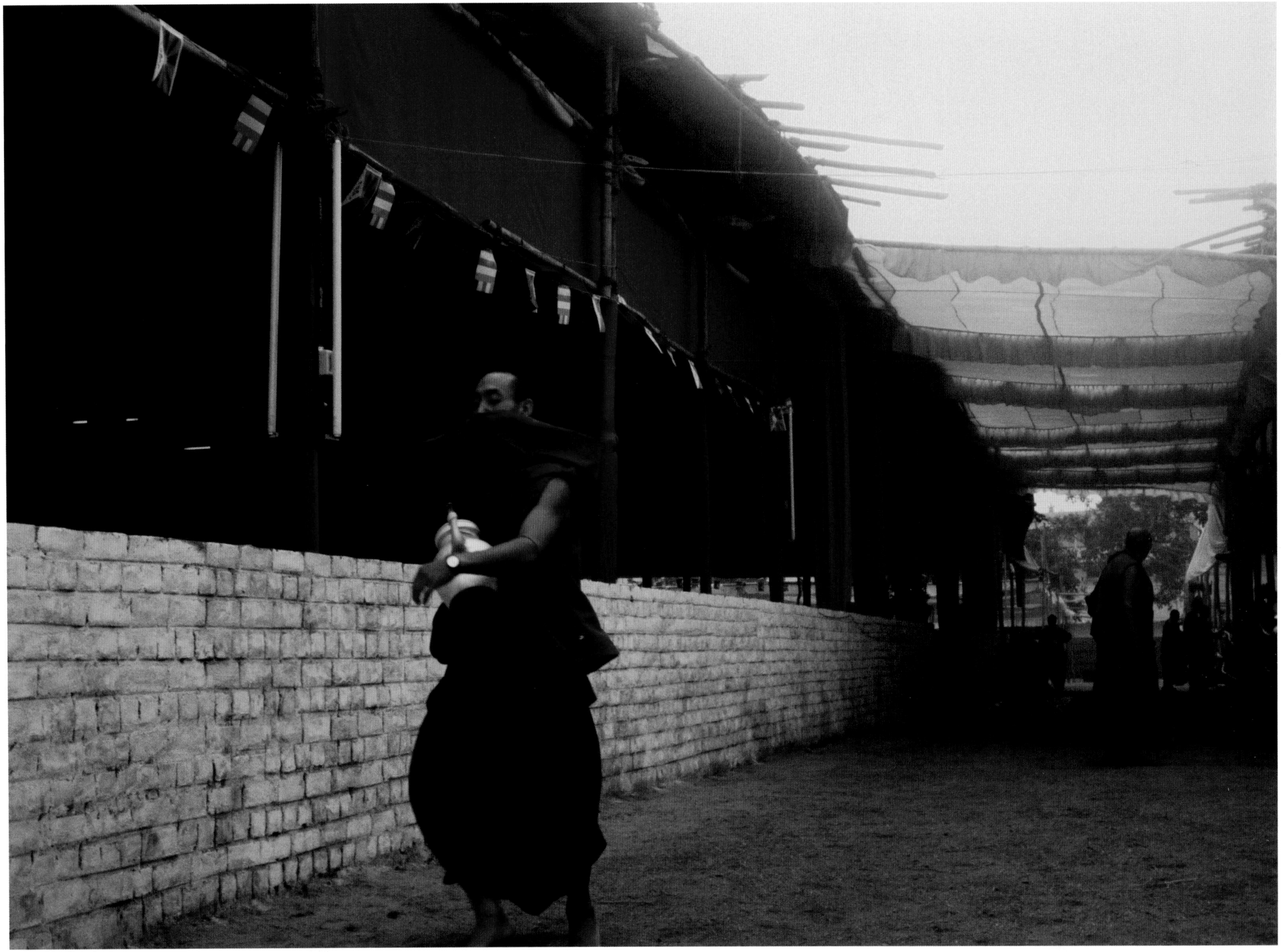

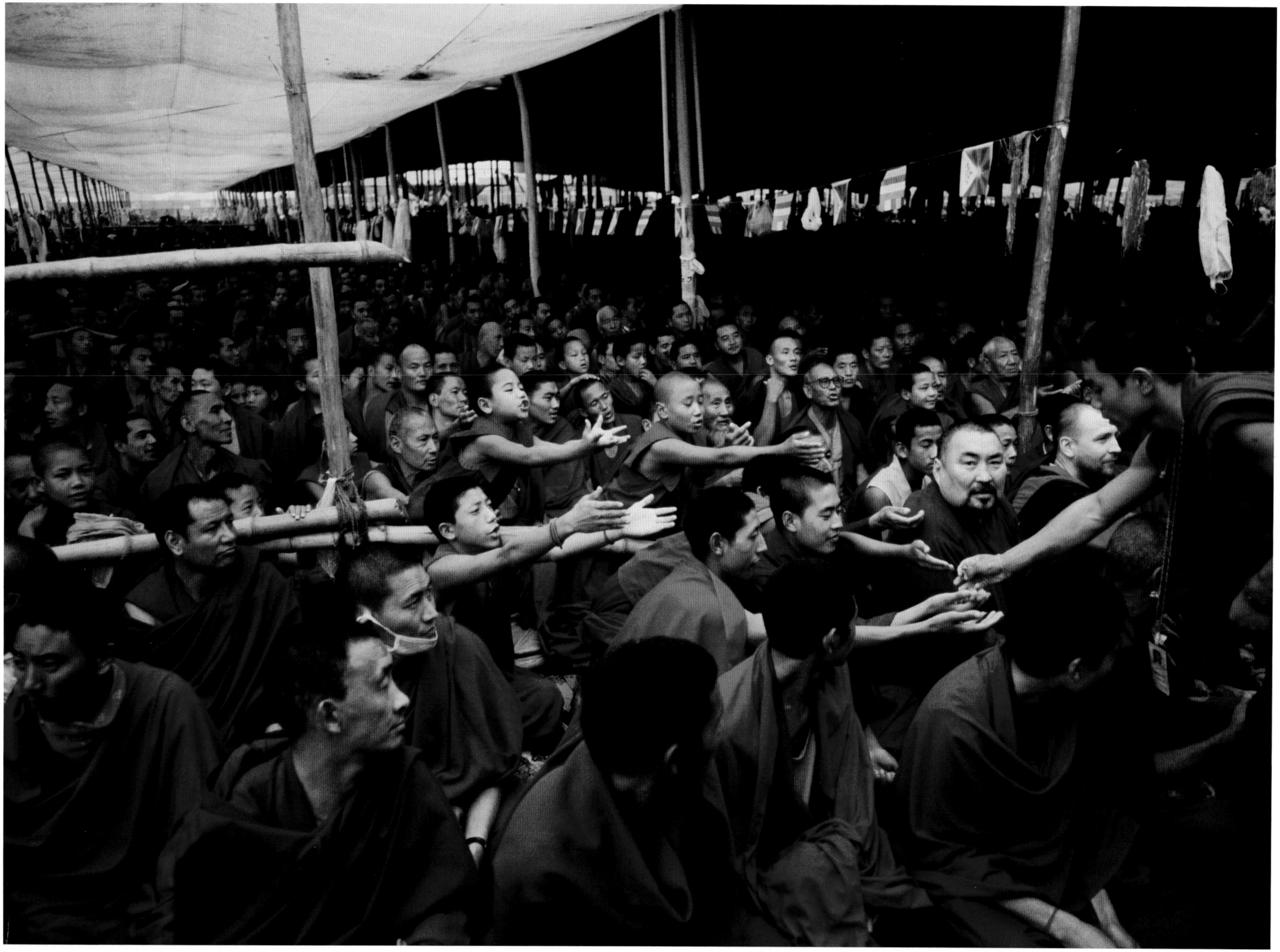

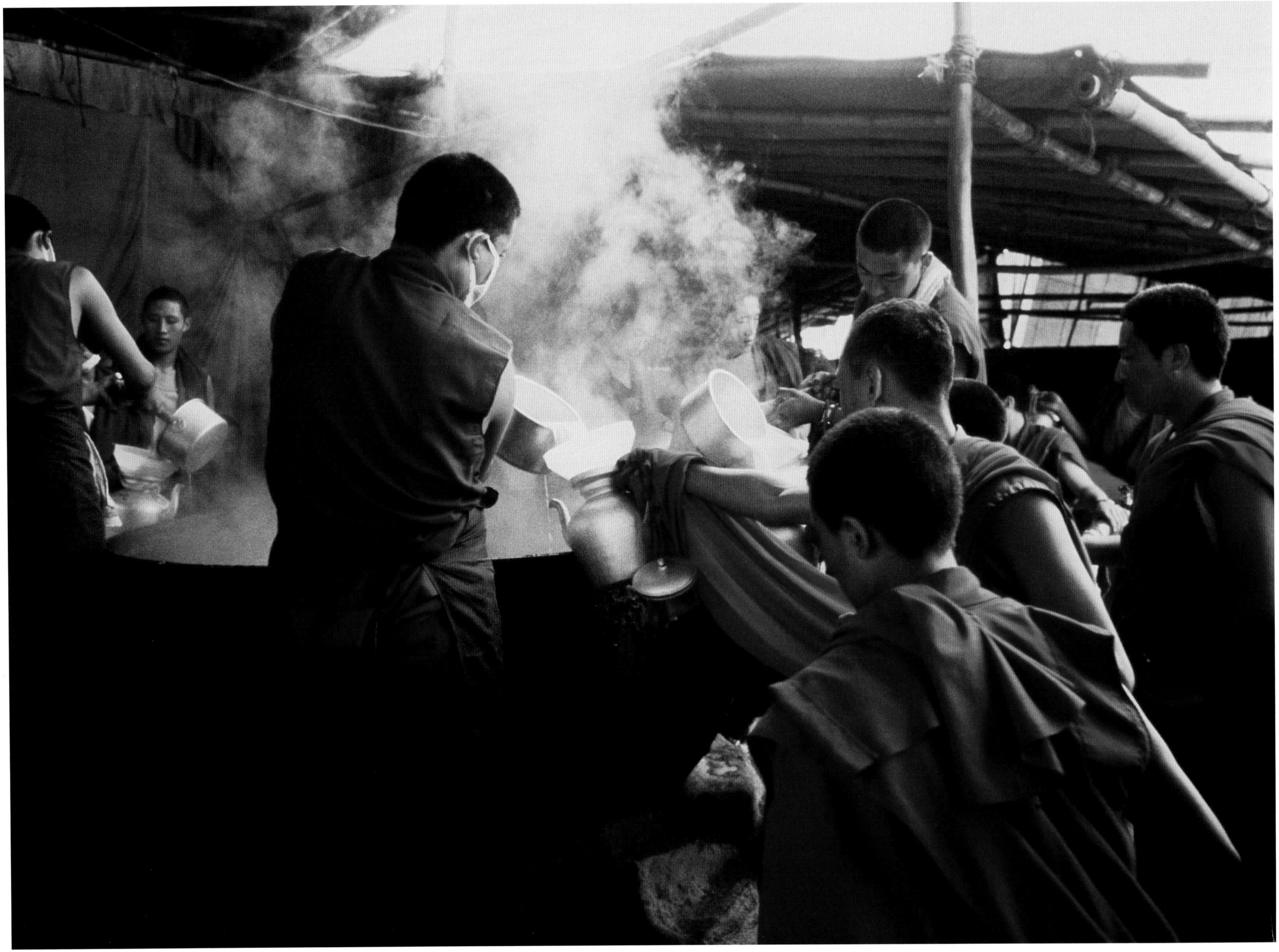

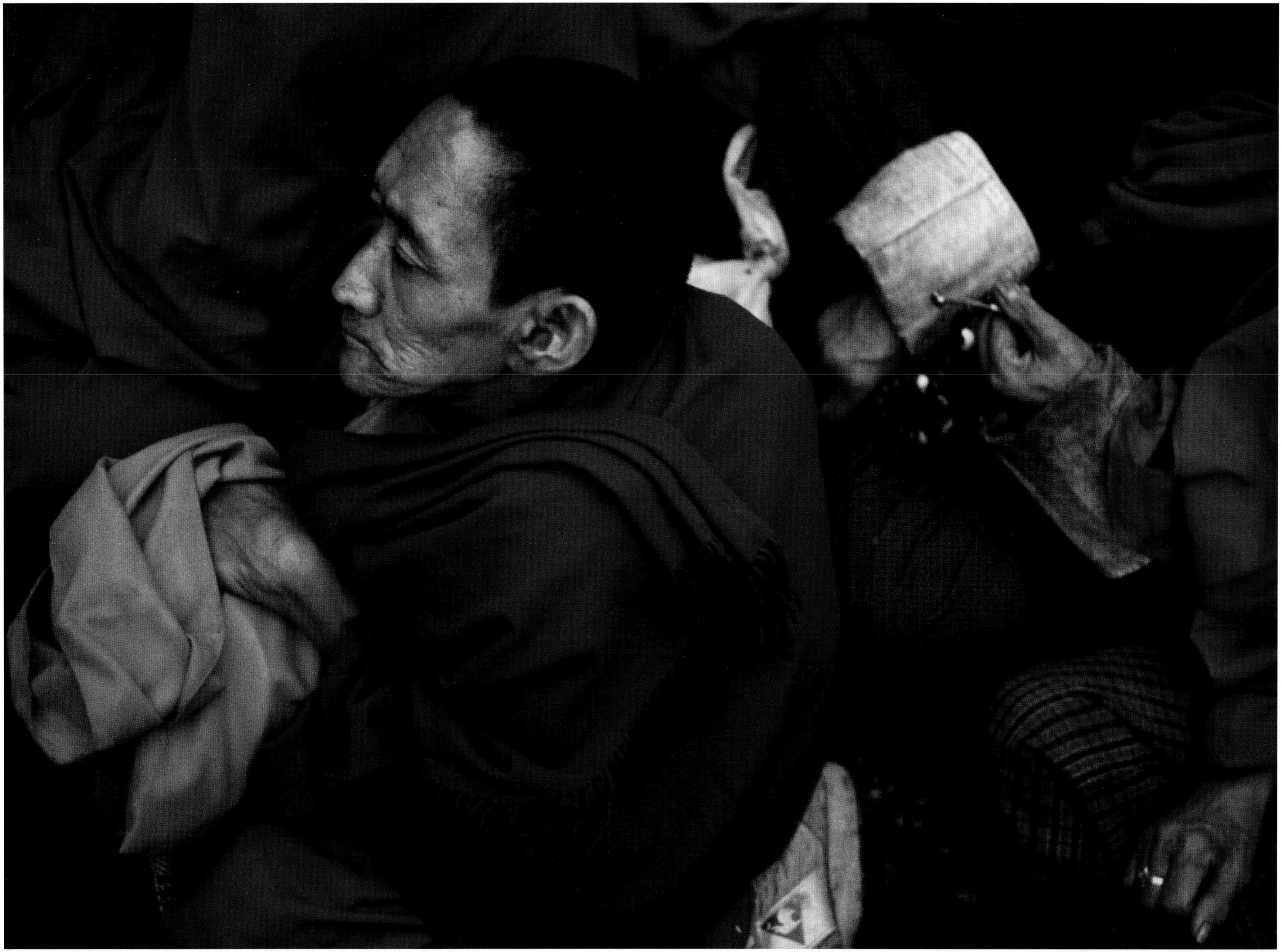

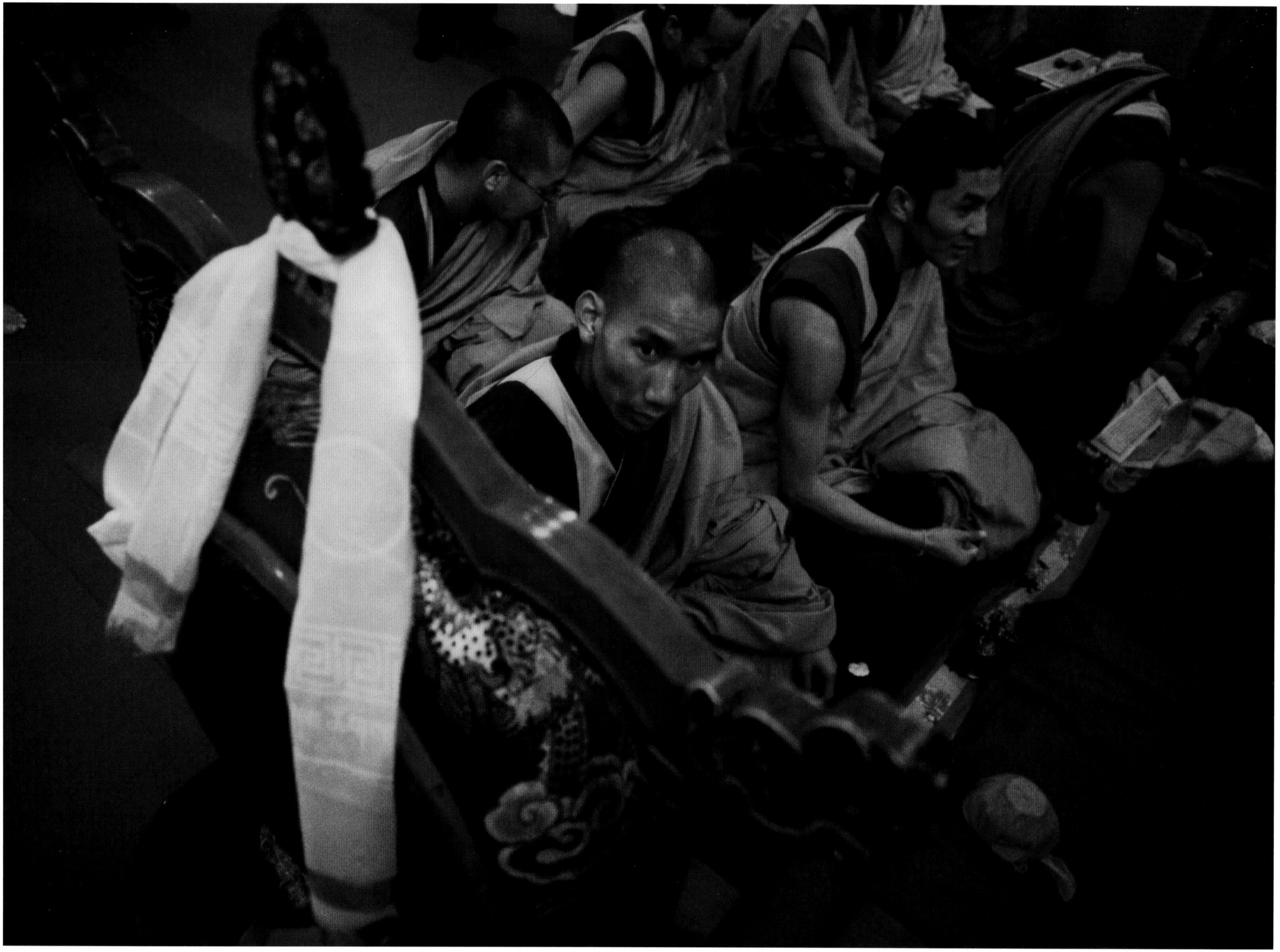

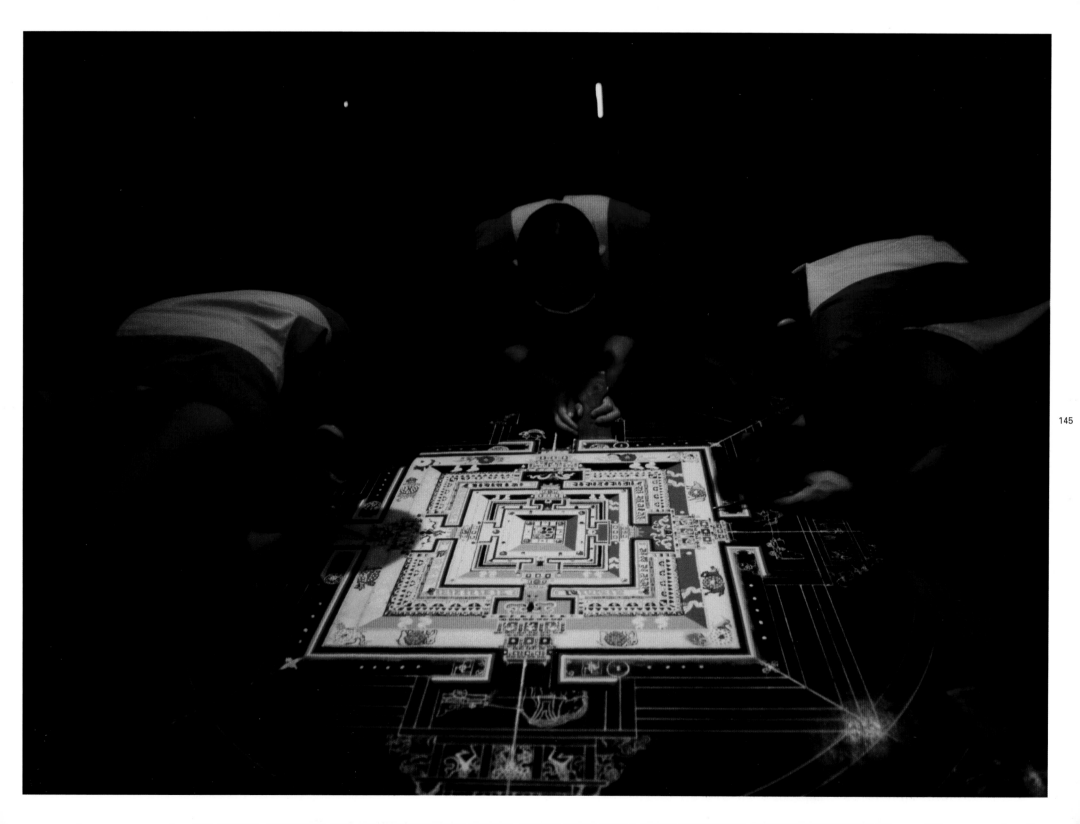

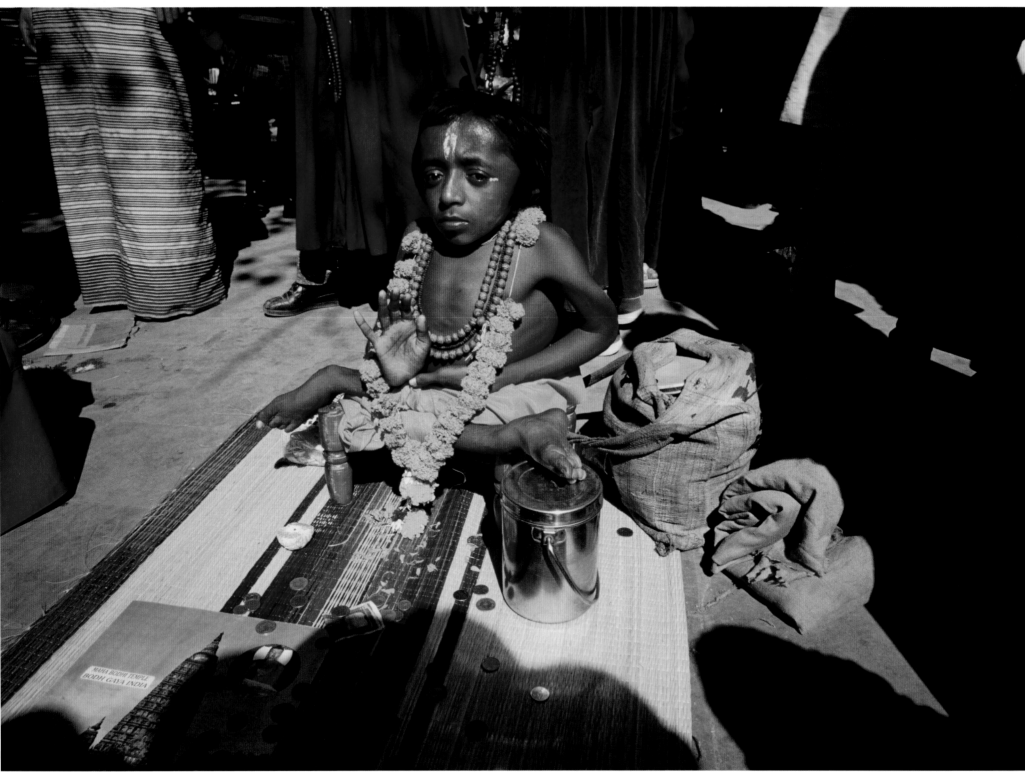